Praise & Wo]
HYMN SOLOS 1

ALTO SAX

15 Hymns Arranged for Solo Performance
by Stan Pethel

HOW TO USE THE CD ACCOMPANIMENT:
A melody cue appears on the right channel only. If your CD player has a balance adjustment, you can adjust the volume of the melody by turning down the right channel.

ISBN 978-0-7935-9756-7

HAL•LEONARD®
CORPORATION

7777 W. BLUEMOUND RD. P.O. BOX 13819 MILWAUKEE, WI 53213

Visit Hal Leonard on the internet at http://www.halleonard.com

2

BLESSED BE THE NAME ◆

ALTO SAX

Traditional

O FOR A THOUSAND TONGUES TO SING
Text by CHARLES WESLEY
Music by CARL G. GLASER

ALTO SAX

Words and Music by
WILLIAM MOORE

4

COME CHRISTIANS JOIN TO SING ◆③

ALTO SAX

Words by CHRISTIAN HENRY BATEMAN
Traditional Melody

COME, THOU FOUNT OF EVERY BLESSING ◆4

Words by ROBERT ROBINSON
Traditional Music compiled by JOHN WYETH

ALTO SAX

FAIREST LORD JESUS ◆5

ALTO SAX

Words for stanza 4 by JOSEPH AUGUST SEISS
Silesian Folk Melody
Arranged by RICHARD STORRS WILLIS

HOLY, HOLY, HOLY ❻

Text by REGINALD HEBER
Music by JOHN B. DYKES

ALTO SAX

I NEED THEE EVERY HOUR ◆7

ALTO SAX

Words by ANNIE S. HAWKS
Music by ROBERT LOWRY

I STAND AMAZED IN THE PRESENCE ◆ 8

Words and Music by
CHARLES H. GABRIEL

ALTO SAX

MY FAITH LOOKS UP TO THEE ◆9

Words by RAY PALMER
Music by LOWELL MASON

ALTO SAX

O WORSHIP THE KING 🔟

Words by ROBERT GRANT
Based on Lyons,
Attributed to JOHANN MICHAEL HAYDN

ALTO SAX

PRAISE TO THE LORD, THE ALMIGHTY ◆11

ALTO SAX

Words by JOACHIM NEANDER
Music from Erneuerten Gesangbuch
Harmony by WILLIAM STERNDALE BENNETT

REJOICE YE PURE IN HEART 12

Words by EDWARD HAYES PLUMPTRE
Music by ARTHUR HENRY MESSITER

ALTO SAX

'TIS SO SWEET TO TRUST IN JESUS

Words by LOUISE M. R. STEAD
Music by WILLIAM J. KIRKPATRICK

ALTO SAX

TO GOD BE THE GLORY ◆14

Words by FANNIE J. CROSBY
Music by WILLIAM H. DOANE

ALTO SAX

WE HAVE HEARD THE JOYFUL SOUND 15

Words by PRISCILLA J. OWENS
Music by WILLIAM J. KIRKPATRICK

ALTO SAX